pp 2.1.1ff.jpg

Prayers Before Meals

by

Anne R. Ford
&
Jeffrey Ford Kovite

Tin Can Press
Myrtle Beach, South Carolina
2015

.

ISBN-13: 978-1515391234
ISBN-10:15139123X

CONTENTS

Daily Prayers Before Meals
January - December

Prayers and Toasts For Special Days
Anniversary
Baptism
Birth
Birthday
Celebration
Confirmation
Engagement
Graduation
New Home
New Year
Retirement
Travel
Wedding

January

January 1

Praise be to you, Lord Jesus Christ. We remember your goodness during the past year, dear Lord, and we thank you for providing for us. We pray for your blessing in this New Year, and ask your mercy, guidance and providence for our country, ourselves and our absent loved ones. In Jesus' name. Amen.

January 2

Heavenly Father, we ask your blessings on the food provided for us this day. Amen

January 3

We give thanks to you, dear Lord, for the gifts we are about to receive. Amen.

January 4

We thank you, Lord for providing for us and ask your blessing as we share our meal this day. Amen

January 5
In your mercy, O Lord, bless the fruit of the
earth you have provided for us. Amen.

January 6
What star is this, with beams so bright
More beauteous than the noonday light?
It shines to herald for the King
And wise men to His crib to bring.
Know we not that little baby
Was the bright and morning Star?

He is King forever, over all to reign.
Gracious Lord, may we evermore be led
to you. Amen.

January 7
Dear God, you have given us food for our
bodies and heavenly food for our souls.
We praise you, dear Lord, for your goodness
to us.
Thanks be to God. Amen.

January 8

Dear Lord, we thank you for the meal we are about to share.
May it strengthen us in mind and body.
Thanks be to God. Amen.

January 9

Our Father in heaven, we are gathered here in your name.
We thank you, Lord, for this meal and for all your gifts.
In Jesus' name. Amen.

January 10

We thank you, heavenly Father, for your goodness.
Bless us and these gifts we are about to receive. Amen.

January 11
Dear Lord, we thank you for our daily bread and for all the blessings you have bestowed on us.
In Jesus' name. Amen.

January 12
Holy Spirit, O God, we give thanks for the nourishment provided for us this day. Lord God, we pray you will nourish our souls with your grace. Amen.

January 13
Lord God, bless the gifts you have given us this day.
Please protect and guide us and keep us ever mindful of your love. Amen.

January 14
We thank you, Lord, for this food and pray we may ever be faithful in serving you.
In Jesus' name. Amen.

January 15
Lord, we ask your blessing on the meal you have provided for us.
Let all the world praise you, heavenly Father. Amen.

January 16
Dear Lord, we thank you for providing food for us this day.
May it strengthen us in mind and body. Amen.

January 17
Bless us, O Lord, and these Thy gifts we are about to receive from Thy bounty.
Through Christ our Lord. Amen.

January 18
O Lord, we ask your blessing on all here present and on the meal we are about to share.
Teach us, O Lord, to share our daily lives with you. Amen.

January 19

Dear God, accept the thanks of our hearts for all the blessings you have bestowed on us. (Each person mention a blessing) Amen.

January 20

Dear Lord, we thank you for food, family and home. We praise you for these blessings. Amen.

January 21

Thank you dear Lord, for our daily bread. Strengthen us, that we may hear your word and be ever close to you. Amen.

January 22

We praise you and love you, O God most high. Be present at our table this day. Bless us, we pray, and the food you have provided for us. Amen.

January 23

The Lord is faithful,
He will establish you and guard you from the evil one.
We give thanks to God for all our blessings. Amen.

January 24

The Lord loves us and has blessed us.
All things work together for good to those who love God.
Praise be to you, Lord Jesus Christ. Amen

January 25

The Lord, our God, has blessed us with His bounty.
Bless us again heavenly Father, that we may ever be faithful to you. Amen.

January 26

Lord, Thou has nourished us with good food.
Help us to live that we may enjoy health of mind and body.
Thanks be to God. Amen.

January 27

Lord, we offer our prayer of thanksgiving to you for the blessings we share at our table this day. Amen.

January 28

Bless these gifts of your bounty, for which we give thanks and praise. Amen.

January 29

Be present at our table, Lord.
Bless us, we pray, and the meal we are about to share.
In Jesus' name. Amen.

January 30
Dear Lord, Bless the meal you have
provided, that it will nourish us with love for
you and for each other. Amen.

January 31
O Lord, we ask your blessing on our meal
and all who partake of it.
Be with us now and forever, we pray. Amen.

February

February 1
Bless us O Lord and these bountiful gifts we are about receive.
Bless us also with peace in this house.
Thanks be to God. Amen.

February 2
May God bless us with the light of love and understanding.
O Lord, bless also the food you have provided for us. Amen.

February 3
Dear Lord, we ask your blessing on all here present and for the gift of food and companionship we are about to partake.
Amen.

February 4

Lord we thank you for the beautiful earth you made which has provided food for us today.
Thanks be to God for His loving care of us. Amen.

February 5

God's grace has protected us.
His love has blessed us.
Bless us again, O Lord, and the fruit of the earth you have provided. Amen.

February 6

Thank you, dear Lord, for the blessings of home and family and for the meal we are about to share. Amen.

February 7

O gracious Lord, we ask your blessing of our meal and for all here present.
Thanks be to God. Amen

February 8
In His wisdom and goodness God gave
mankind the earth and its bounty.
Lord, we are thankful for your loving
kindness in providing this meal for us.
Amen.

February 9
Bless us, O Lord, with happy hearts and
bless this house and our meal.
We ask this in Jesus' name. Amen.

February 10
O Lord God, help us to love one another as
you love us.
Make us patient and understanding of each
other.
Bless us, dear Lord, and the gifts prepared
for us to share. Amen.

February 11

Lord, fill our hearts with your grace that we may truly appreciate one another.

We pray, dear Lord, to bless us and the meal we are about to share. Amen.

February 12 - President Lincoln's Birthday

In an 1863 speech, Abraham Lincoln said, "It is the duty of nations as well as of men to acknowledge their dependence upon God." Acknowledging this, let us now ask God's blessing on our country:

We thank you, Lord, for this land and for the freedom that is our heritage.

We ask you ,Lord, to protect the families of this nation, guard our children and have mercy on us all that we may always act according to your will. Amen.

February 13
O Lord, bless this meal and those gathered here.
Through Christ our Lord. Amen

February 14 - St. Valentine's Day
With praise for God's wonderful gift of love, let us honor good St.Valentine, and thank God for all our blessings. Amen (each person mentions a blessing.)

February 15
Lord, grant your blessing to all here present.
For our daily bread, dear Lord, we thank you. Amen.

February 16
Heavenly Father, by your hand we are fed.
Thank you, dear Lord, for this food we are about to receive.
Bless and strengthen us that we may live according to your Word. Amen.

February 17
Dear Lord we thank you for these blessings, for the food provided for us this day, and all those we share it with.
Through Christ our Lord, Amen.

February 18
We thank you, dear Lord, as we gather around the table, for the blessing of our meal and the joys we shared this day.
Thanks be to God. Amen.

February 19
Thank you, dear Lord, for caring for our daily needs by providing us with food and shelter, home and family.
Thanks be to God. Amen.

February 20
Dear Lord, we ask your blessing on all here present and on the gift of food we are about to share. Amen.

February 21

O God, you who have fed our bodies with daily bread and our souls with the Bread of Salvation, hear our prayers of praise and thanksgiving for your loving care of us. Thanks be to you, almighty and everlasting God, creator of heaven and earth. Amen.

February 22 - Washington's Birthday

Today we honor the first president of our country, George Washington.

During the Revolutionary War, General Washington prayed daily, often kneeling in the snow, asking God for guidance and the strength to persevere through the suffering of many years of war that freed our country from tyranny.

May the principles he lived by be enshrined in our hearts and God grant we keep safe this country. Amen.

February 23
Thanks be to God for He has blessed us with all good things. Amen.

February 24
Lord, you fed the multitude with 5 loaves and 2 fishes.
You have fed us also with your bounty and your word.
Thanks be to God. Amen.

February 25
Praise be to God.
He has blessed us with every good thing.
We thank you Lord, for your loving care.
Amen.

February 26
Let us to be ever mindful of God's goodness, for He has nourished our bodies and souls, hearts and minds.
Thanks be to God. Amen

February 27
Bless us, through Christ our Lord, for this bounty and accept our thanks and praise. Amen.

February 28
Praise be to you, Lord Jesus Christ, son of the Eternal Father.
You have strengthened our souls with the bread of heaven and our bodies with good food.
Thanks be to God. Amen

February 29 (Leap Year)
Thanks be to God for fulfilling our daily needs.
We praise you for your goodness this day and ask for your blessing. Amen.

March

March 1

May the Holy Spirit live in us and help us to follow the Lord, who has blessed us this day.

Thanks be to God for all his blessings.

Amen.

March 2

We thank you, Lord, for your blessings.

Dear God, continue to bless us as we prepare and partake of this meal.

In Jesus' name. Amen.

March 3

Dear God, you are the author of liberty, who loves us and provides for us.

Bless us again we pray, Lord. Amen

March 4

Dear God, you have been our help through the ages.

Bless us and direct our paths through life.

In Jesus' name we pray. Amen.

March 5

God provides for us throughout our lives.
We beg you, O Lord God, to bestow your
blessing on us all. Amen.

March 6

Teach us your ways, O Lord, that we may
follow you.
Bless us, O Lord, with love of family and
country.
Thanks be to God. Amen.

March 7

The Lord is God of all. Him we worship
and Him we obey.
God's blessing remains with us as we thank
Him for his loving care this day. Amen.

March 8

All your works proclaim your praise, O
Lord, earth and sea and sky.
You are God, the loving Father of us all.
We ask your blessing on all here present.
In Jesus' name, Amen.

March 9

O God of distant ages.
O God now present with us today.
You are everlasting.
We praise you and love you and ask your
mercy and blessing this day. Amen.

March 10

You have blessed us this day with our daily
bread, O Lord.
Keep us ever mindful of your loving care of
us, dear God. Amen.

March 11

God has shed his Grace on our country and its people.
Let us be true to Him in all ways.
Bless us O Lord with faithful hearts.
In Jesus' name we pray. Amen.

March 12

Sing to the Lord with a cheerful voice.
God is faithful, true and loving.
We thank you, Lord, for your blessings.
Amen

March 13

Lord God, you have blessed us with the gifts of home, the love of family and friends and the dignity of work.
Bless also this gift of food we are about to consume.
We thank you for all these wondrous gifts.
Amen.

March 14

Your word O Lord, finds a home in our hearts.
Bless us with courage and a strong faith.
Bless our food, O Lord we pray, that we will be strengthened and nourished.
In Jesus' name. Amen.

March 15

Lord make us a witness to your truth and strengthen our faith.
Bless us, we beseech you, and the food you have provided for us this day.
Thanks be to God. Amen

March 16

Blessed be God.
Blessed be His Holy Name.
Blessed be all of us with health of mind and body. Amen

March 17 - St. Patrick's Day

Teach us to follow St. Patrick 's courage, and learn to protect the faith you have given to us.

St. Patrick made Ireland the land of saints and scholars, faithful in all things.

Let us honor and bless St. Patrick this day. Amen.

March 18

Teach us to be mindful of our blessings, O Lord.

Watch over us and keep us from sin and harm.

Bless our meal this day. Amen.

March 19

Dear Lord, we ask your blessing this day on us, our family, our friends and the meal we are about to share. Thanks be to God. Amen.

March 20
Dear God, bless us, we pray, and this meal
that you have so generously provided.
In Jesus' name, we thank Thee. Amen.

March 21
O God, protect us from all evil and bring us
to everlasting life.
Bless us this day and bless this meal.
In Jesus' name, we ask Thee. Amen

March 22
Praise be to our Heavenly Father, who loves
us and has blessed us with all good things.
Thanks be to God. Amen.

March 23
Dear Lord, we thank you for another day.
Help us to live well and be mindful of our
blessings as we gather together to eat this
meal.
We ask Thy blessing on us, O Lord. Amen.

March 24
Sing to the Lord for he has loved us and daily blesses us with good food.
Thanks be to God. Amen.

March 25
Glory and praise to God who alone gives light to our days.
Many are the blessings He has given us.
In Jesus' name. Amen.

March 26
Thank you dear Lord for the gifts of food and drink that we shall share this day.
Thanks be to God. Amen.

March 27
Blessed are we, O Lord, who gather together to eat this meal you have provided for us.
In Jesus' name. Amen.

March 28

Praise be to you, O Lord, for the friendship and love at our table.
You have blessed us with all good things.
In Jesus' name. Amen.

March 29

Most gracious and heavenly Father, thank you for this food that is prepared for the nourishment of our bodies.
Through Christ, Our Lord. Amen

March 30

Dear Jesus, you have given us the Bread of Life.
Sustain us also, we pray, that we may grow in spiritual faith and physical well being.
Glory be to God. Amen.

March 31
May the Father, Son and Holy Spirit bless each of us this day and watch over us as we work, play, study and sleep. Amen.

April

April 1
Lord, let your light shine upon us and give us peace.
We thank you for the food that you have provided, for our good health, for love of family and the friends we are blessed with.
In Jesus' name. Amen.

April 2
For family, friends, love and food, we thank you this day O Lord. Amen.

April 3
You have given us our daily bread, O gracious Lord, and we thank you for this blessing.
In Jesus' name, Amen.

April 4
The heavens proclaim your splendor, O Lord God.
Let us praise you and thank you for our blessings. Amen.

April 5

Dear Lord, let it be our mission to serve you better as we grow in grace.
Bless our home and the homes of loved ones gathered around this table, we pray. Amen.

April 6

All good things come from you, O Lord.
We thank you for your loving care.
Bless us and this meal you have provided to nourish us this day.
In Jesus' name, Amen.

April 7

Dear God, we thank you for this food.
Make us conscious of your grace in our lives each day.
In Jesus' name. Amen.

April 8

O God, look upon us and bless us this day
we pray Thee.
Bless our family and our food as we gather
together to give thanks.
Thanks be to God. Amen.

April 9

O Lord, make us thankful for the meal we
are about to enjoy.
Bless us and keep us mindful of your
goodness to us.
In Jesus' name we pray. Amen.

April 10

Lord we thank you for the daily bread you
have provided for us.
Feed us also with love to nourish our spirits.
Amen.

April 11

Thank you, dear Lord, for the beautiful world you have given to us.
Keep us mindful of you, the creator and our Heavenly Father, who loves us and has given us all good things.
In Jesus' name. Amen.

April 12

May we all rest in God's presence, confident in His love.
We thank you, Lord, for all the blessings you have bestowed on us.
Thanks be to God. Amen.

April 13

We are the children of God, the creator of heaven and earth.
He has provided for us each day.
We thank Him and praise Him, the Almighty God. Amen.

April 14

Dear Lord, accept our thanks this day for the meal you have provided for us.
Bless us, we pray, and keep us ever mindful of your everlasting love. Amen.

April 15

For our daily food, we thank you, O God, and for family and friends and home.
We ask your blessing on all gathered here today. Amen.

April 16

You have fed our bodies with all that is good, dear Lord.
May our minds and hearts and souls be nourished with the knowledge of your love.
Thanks be to Almighty God. Amen.

May 5

Lord, we acknowledge our dependence on you, for you are the source of all life. Bless us, we pray. Amen.

May 6

O Lord, make us mindful of the beauty of the earth you created.
Teach us to appreciate the little things that blossom and bloom and make our world beautiful.
In Jesus' name we pray. Amen.

May 7

May God's love light our way as we go about our daily chores and may He bless this meal with His presence.
Come, Lord Jesus, be with us at our table.
In the name of Christ, our Lord. Amen.

May 8
Dear God, you are the past, present and future.
Bless us and guide us on our journey.
O Lord, hear our prayer. Amen.

May 9
Dear Lord, grant us your merciful bounty and ceaseless grace as we gather together here this day. Amen.

May 10
Let us give all our thanks to you, O Lord, for this nourishing meal so it may sustain our lives and love for you. Amen.

May 11
Bless this food, O Lord, and grant that our souls be nourished by your gracious gift of love. Amen.

May 12

Heavenly father, accept these thanks for the gifts we are about to receive.
Help us live our lives as you would want.
Praise be to God. Amen.

May 13

Thank you, God, for this bounty.
Keep us in the light of your love and watch over us every day. Amen.

May 14

O God, we need your love and your light.
May we bask in your golden glow forever more.
Thanks be to God. Amen.

May 15

Accept our gratitude, O Lord, and keep us within your guiding light, free from harm.
Praise the Lord. Amen

May 16

Thank you Lord for all we have and all we need.
Grant us the strength to live as Christians should.
Amen.

May 17

Dear Lord, we pray for your forgiveness and love.
Accept also these prayers of thanks and praise to you, O God.
Amen.

May 18

Thanks be to the Lord, from whom all nourishment flows.
We praise Thee, Lord. Amen.

May 19

Please accept these prayers of gratitude for this meal, O Lord, and grant us good health in body and soul. Amen

May 20
Bless us O Lord, with your light of love and understanding that we may live together in peace.
Thanks be to God. Amen.

May 21
Thanks be to God for health of mind and body and for the meal prepared for us this day. Amen.

May 22
God's grace has protected us and His love has blessed us.
Thanks be to God. Amen.

May 23
Gracious Lord, we ask your blessing upon us and this meal we are about to receive.
Through Christ our Lord. Amen

May 24

God has given the earth and its bounty to mankind.
Lord God, we thank you for your providence and ask for your guidance that we will use earth's resources wisely. Amen

May 25

Lord, bless this house we pray.
Give happy and loving hearts to all who dwell here.
Thanks be to God. Amen.

May 26

Dear Lord, bless us and these Thy gifts we are about to enjoy.
Through Christ our Lord, Amen.

May 27
Dear Lord, bless our land with peace and
prosperity.
Bless us also with clean and thankful hearts.
We pray Thee Lord. Amen.

May 28
Dear Lord, help us to keep our lives firmly
directed toward you and to be mindful of all
our blessings. Amen

May 30
Lord, we ask your blessing on us this day as
we gather around this feast.
We thank you for your loving care of us.
Amen.

May 31
Thank you, Lord, for all your gifts and
especially for this meal.
Praise be to God. Amen

June

June 1

Dear God, we give you thanks for all we have received from your bounty.
In Jesus' name. Amen.

June 2

For all our blessings we thank you Lord.
Grant that we may always be mindful of your love. Amen.

June 3

We thank you Lord for your loving care of us.
In Jesus' name please bless our daily bread.
Amen.

June 4

You have provided this meal for us, O Lord.
For this and all our blessings, we thank you.
Amen.

June 5

Our Father in heaven, you are the living God who watches over us and guides us. Praise be to you, Lord God of all. Amen

June 6

We know that all blessings come from you, O Lord.
You have blessed us with this food and we thank you for your gentle care. Amen

June 7

Let us pray together in thanksgiving for all the blessings God has bestowed on us. In Jesus' name, we thank you, Lord. Amen

June 8

For what we are about to receive, we thank you, dear Lord.
Amen

June 9
We praise God for His blessings.
Lord, bless our home we pray and bless our meal this day.
In Jesus' name, we praise the Lord. Amen.

June 10
Bless us, O Lord, and these Thy gifts we are about to receive from Thy bounty through Christ our Lord. Amen

June 11
Lord, we pray, bless our family, our home and the meal you have provided for us. In Jesus' name. Amen.

June 12
We thank you, O Lord, for your goodness. Bless us, we pray. Amen.

June 13
We ask for your blessing Lord for this meal and in our lives.
Grant us peace and love for each other.
Amen.

June 14 - Arbor Day
The earth is the Lord's and we thank Him on Arbor Day for His gift of trees.
Trees give us shelter, shade, and beauty.
We plant them and take care of them, but only God can make a tree.
We thank Him for the wonderful gift of trees.
Praise be to you, Lord Jesus Christ. Amen.

June 15
Dear Lord, we thank you for this meal.
Bless our food that it will nourish us.
Strengthen our faith, Lord, we pray. Amen.

June 16

Dear God, we ask your blessing on all here present and on the meal we are about to share.
Thanks be to God. Amen.

June 17

O Lord, we are thankful for this meal that you have provided for us this day.
May we be ever mindful of your generous blessings. Amen.

June 18

Heavenly Father, look upon this table and all here present.
Bless us all, we pray, dear Lord. Amen.

June 19

O Lord, every day we ask you for our daily bread and you have supplied our needs.
Make us truly thankful for all our blessings. In Jesus' name we pray. Amen.

June 20

O Lord, our God, you have blessed us with the meal we are about to receive.
We thank you for your continued goodness to us. Amen.

June 21

O Lord, you have provided abundantly for us each day.
Thank you for all our blessings. Amen.

June 22

Dear God, giver of all good gifts, we thank you for the blessings of this meal our family shares. Amen.

June 23

Your blessings, dear Lord, have fed our body and souls.
Preserve us and guide us, we pray. Amen.

June 24

Dear God, we thank you for the daily gift of the food we share.
Keep us close to you, O Lord, we pray.
Amen.

June 25

Dear Lord, accept our thanks for your goodness to us.
Bless us, we pray, with a firm faith.
We ask this through Christ our Lord. Amen.

June 26

Bless us, O Lord, and these Thy gifts we are about to receive from Thy bounty. Amen.

June 27

Blessed are Thou, Lord of Heaven and Earth.
You have blessed us with family, friends and food.
Thanks be to God. Amen.

June 28

Let us be aware of the greatness of God who made this wonderful world. Amen.

June 29

Lord God, you are our shining light throughout our darkest days.
Hear our prayers and lead us in truth.
Praise be to you, dear Lord.
Bless all here present as we pray. Amen.

June 30

Lord, You remain constant, today and always, our loving Father in heaven.
You are He who made the world.
We pray for your blessing of our daily bread.
Thanks be to the everlasting Lord. Amen.

July

July 1

Lord, we ask your blessing on all here at this table and for the food we are about to share. Thanks be to God. Amen.

July 2

We thank you, Lord, for providing for our needs.
In the name of our Savior, Jesus, we pray you will bless our home and all who dwell within. Amen.

July 3

We pray dear God, for your blessing on us and on the fruits of the earth we are about to share.
Through Christ our Lord. Amen.

July 4 - Independence Day
Lord God, you have blessed our country
with freedom of speech, religion, press and
assembly, with opportunity and the pursuit
of happiness for all.
Strengthen us, Lord God, to preserve our
heritage against those who would cause
harm to our nation.
We know eternal vigilance is the price of
liberty.

My country 'tis of Thee
Sweet Land of Liberty
Of Thee I sing
Land where my fathers died,
Land of the Pilgrims pride
From every mountainside
Let freedom ring.

July 5

O gracious God, let us remember you in our hearts and live as you would have us live. Thanks be to God. Amen.

July 6

All praise be to you, Lord, for the precious gifts of love and laughter as we gather for this meal. Amen.

July 7

We praise you Lord for your everlasting love and merciful forgiveness. Amen.

July 8

Eternal praise be to you, O God.
We strive towards the light of your love and ask for your blessings. Amen.

July 9

Bless these precious gifts and grant us love and peace as we praise you and thank you, O Lord. Amen.

July 10
Dear Lord, we accept these gifts and give praise to you.
Grant us your mercy and love evermore.
Amen.

July 11
Lord God of all, hear these prayers of praise and thanks for this meal before us. Thanks be to God. Amen.

July 12
Jesus, Son of God, please accept our praise and thanks for all that we have before us.
Amen.

July 13
Lord, we ask your blessing on all here present and on the food provided at this meal.
Thanks be to God. Amen.

July 14

Lord, grant us your blessing as we go about this day.
Bless also those around our table and the meal we are about to share.
Lord, hear our prayer. Amen.

July 15

Lord, we are your children.
We pray for your blessing on our home and family as we share the joys and cares of life.
More joys than cares, we pray Thee Lord. Amen.

July 16

Lord we thank you for your loving care.
We pray you will bless us and our meal this day.
May we always walk in the light of your love. Amen.

July 17

Lord God Almighty, we worship and praise you for you are Lord of heaven and earth. Grant us your blessing this day.
Through Christ our Lord we pray. Amen.

July 18

Everlasting Father, we pray for your blessing on all here present and for this meal. In Jesus' name, the name above all other names, we pray Thee. Amen.

July 19

Dear God, we ask your blessing. Enlighten us that we may love you and keep your Word.
Help us and enlighten us that we may make the world a better place.
In the name of the Blessed Trinity, we pray. Amen.

July 20

Dear Lord, bless this house and all here present as we share this meal.
We ask this through Jesus Christ our Lord. Amen.

July 21

O God, grant your blessing upon us and the food we are about to receive.
Through Christ our Lord. Amen.

July 22

Lord, we pray for your blessing this day.
Come in to our hearts and minds, O Holy Spirit of God, that we may live in Thee. Amen.

July 23

Almighty God, we ask your blessing on all here present.
Keep us in health of mind and body, we pray.
Through Christ our Lord. Amen.

July 24

Lord, in this season of harvest, we ask your blessing for all farmers and for the land that it may be fruitful.

Bless us also, we pray, and the meal we are about to partake.

Thanks be to God. Amen.

July 25

Lord, we know every good gift is from you. We give thanks for home, family and food and for your care of us. Amen.

July 26

Bless us, dear Lord, and your gracious gifts that we are about to receive.

Through Jesus Christ our Lord. Amen.

July 27

Holy God, you fed with manna our forefathers wandering in the desert.
Feed us, we pray, with your blessing for the food provided this day.
Through Christ our Lord. Amen.

July 28

Dear Lord, we trust in you to provide our needs.
You are our comfort and our strength.
Bless us, Lord, and the food we are about to receive. Thanks be to God. Amen

July 29

Lord God, Creator blest, we acknowledge our dependence on you, our loving Father.
We are created in your image and know that you love us.
Praise be to you, Lord Jesus Christ. Amen.

July 30

Heaven and earth declare your glory, Lord.
You are the creator of all things.
Please create in us a heart of love for you,
wondrous Lord, who cares for all his
creatures. Amen.

July 31

Praise the Lord, for He is good.
His blessing is upon us this day.
Thanks be to God. Amen.

August

August 1
Let us count our blessings.
God blesses us each day.
We thank Him for His goodness and ask His blessing on this meal.
Through Christ our Lord. Amen.

August 2
God is faithful, true and loving to His people.
We thank the Lord for His wonderful care of us.
Bless us this day and the meal we are about to share.
Through Christ our Lord. Amen.

August 3
Dear Lord, You have sustained us with our daily bread and we give thanks for our blessings.
In Jesus' name, we pray. Amen.

August 4

We give thanks to God our Father, for all his blessings.
May God's justice reign on earth as it does in heaven.
Thanks be to God. Amen.

August 5

Give thanks to the Lord for His eternal mercy and love.
For all our blessings, we thank you Lord.
In Jesus' name. Amen.

August 6

Dear Lord, we ask your blessing for all here present and the meal provided for us this day,
Thanks be to God. Amen.

August 7
Thanks be to you, Almighty God, for the
food provided for us this day.
For all our blessings, Lord, make us truly
grateful. Amen.

August 8
Blessed be the Lord for He has provided for
us this day.
Thanks be to God. Amen.

August 9
Let us praise the Lord and forget not his
goodness.
God loves us and blesses us. Amen.

August 10
O faithful Lord, watch over us, protect us
from sin and harm.
Bless our home and family, we pray.
In Jesus' name. Amen.

August 11

We give thanks, dear God, for your goodness to us.
You have provided us with all good things.
In Jesus' name we thank you and ask your blessing on our dinner. Amen.

August 12

Lord, we are thankful to know you watch over us at work, school, home or play. Be with us, dear Lord, for we need your blessing.
In Jesus' name we pray. Amen.

August 13

Blessed are Thou, Lord of heaven and earth.
We thank you for our daily bread.
Thanks be to God. Amen.

August 14

Holy Spirit, come into our hearts.
Make us your own.
Guide us on life's paths and bless all
gathered here and the meal we will share.
Through Christ our Lord. Amen.

August 15

Lord, we pray for your blessing this day, for
all here present and for the meal we are
about to share.
Thanks be to God for His loving kindness to
us. Amen.

August 16

Lord, you have blessed us with all that is
good.
Thanks be to God for these blessings.
In Jesus' name we pray. Amen.

August 17
Lord, keep us at peace we pray.
Keep our minds on pure and happy thoughts.
Bless our bodies with good food and good health.
Thanks be to God. Amen.

August 18
Lord, we rejoice in the beauty of the world you have made.
Bless us with your light that we may live according to your Word.
In Jesus' name, we pray. Amen.

August 19
Bless us all near and far, dear Lord, and the meal provided for us this day.
Thanks be to God. Amen.

August 20

Give thanks to God for life, for health of
mind and body, for food and drink, for
work, for sleep and relaxation.
For everything in life we give thanks.
In Jesus' name. Amen.

August 21

Dear Lord, each day we ask your blessing
on our daily bread.
Thank you, God, for hearing our prayer and
sustaining us.
In Jesus' name. Amen.

August 22

We ask your blessing on our meal, Lord, and
beseech you with our prayers.
Thanks be to God, His mercy is everlasting.
Amen.

August 23
Lord, you said "Ask and Ye shall receive".
We, your children, ask your blessing on us
and on this meal we are about to share.
Through Christ our Lord. Amen.

August 24
Dear Lord, accept our thanks for the gifts of
family, friends and food.
We love you, Lord, and are thankful for our
blessings. Amen.

August 25
Dear God, through Jesus Christ, your Son,
you brought salvation to the world.
We give you praise and glory for this
wondrous gift.
Thanks be to God for He has blessed His
people. Amen.

August 26

We pray to you, Lord, to keep us close to you.
Life is too hard to bear alone.
Without you, life would be a desert.
Blessed be God, who is as near as our thoughts.
Through Christ our Lord. Amen.

August 27

Heavenly Father, we give thanks for peace and plenty in our land and in our home. You have blessed us and we thank you, dear God. Amen

August 28

Lord, strengthen us to carry out what we know to be good and right, to promote justice and goodness in the world.
Bless us, we pray, and all unable to be here.
Through Christ our Lord. Amen.

August 29

We, your children, Lord ask your blessings on our home and family this day and on the meal provided for us.
In Jesus' name we pray. Amen.

August 30

Thanks be to God for the nourishment we are about to receive. Amen.

August 31

Accept our thanks, dear Lord, for this day and for this meal.
We praise you for sustaining us through the years.
Thanks be to God. Amen.

September

September 1
We give thanks to the Lord God for His goodness.
Let us ask a blessing for the meal we are about to receive.
Thanks be to God. Amen.

September 2
Praise the Lord, for He is good.
His love has provided for us this day.
Thanks be to God. Amen.

September 3
Lord, you art our refuge and our strength.
Grant us your blessing as we gather around the table to receive our meal. Amen.

September 4
We thank you, Lord, for providing for all our needs. You have blessed our home and nourished our family. Thanks be to God. Amen.

September 5
Bless us, dear Lord, and these bountiful gifts for which we are ever grateful. Amen.

September 6
We pray to you, Lord, for the strength of mind and body to do your work, keep your Word and provide for our family.
Bless us all, we pray. Amen.

September 7
We open our hearts to the Lord to ask His blessing on all here present and the meal provided this day.
Through Christ our Lord. Amen.

September 8
Lord, grant us your blessing this day as we gather for our meal.
Thanks be to God. Amen.

September 9

We are all children of God, made in His image and likeness.
Heavenly Father, bless all your children.
We pray to you. Amen.

September 10

Dear Lord, we ask your blessing for our home and the sustenance provided for us this day.
Thanks be to God. Amen.

September 11

The Lord is our shepherd, we shall not want.
With God as our shepherd, we need not fear.
We pray to Him with confidence, asking His blessing this day. Amen.

September 12
Dear God, as the school year begins, please bless the teachers.
May they inspire young minds to search for truth and love of learning.
In Jesus' name we pray. Amen

September 13
Lord, school has begun.
Keep all children safe from harm.
Help parents give their children loving discipline and guidance.
In Jesus' name we pray. Amen

September 14
Dear Lord, you have called us to love and forgive each other.
We thank you always for giving us a road back to you.
Bless our home and all our travels, we pray.
Thanks be to God. Amen.

September 15

Give thanks to the Lord for He is good.
We ask His blessing on our home this day
and the meal we are about to receive. Amen.

September 16

We have prayed to the Lord for our daily
bread and He has provided for us.
In Him is our trust and love.
Thanks be to God for His goodness. Amen

September 17

Lord, we pray for the blessing of health of
mind and body, for peace in our home and
country.
We thank you for the nourishment provided
this day. Amen.

September 18
Dear God, we ask your blessing on all here present and our loved ones far away. Bless our meal, we pray.
Through Christ our Lord. Amen.

September 19
Lord, you have brought salvation to all who believe in you.
Thanks be to God for this wonderful gift.
Praise to Thee, Almighty God. Amen.

September 20
Thank you, blessed Savior, for your everlasting and loving care.
You have provided all our needs and blessed our home and family.
Thanks be to God. Amen

September 21

Heavenly Father, we give thanks for your goodness.
We ask your blessing on all we lave and who loves us.
Thanks be to God. Amen.

September 22

Lord, you have strengthened us each day with your gift of food.
Bless us again this day, we pray. Amen.

September 23

Lord, bless us. Help us to keep your Word.
Grant us peace and protection.
In Jesus' name. Amen.

September 24

How wonderful it is to know that God, in his heaven, loves us and watches over us.
Thanks be to you, Lord of creation. Amen.

September 25
Almighty Father, giver of all good things,
bless this meal and all gathered here.
We pray to you. Amen.

September 26
Dear Lord, look on us here gathered for
dinner.
We ask for your blessing on us and the meal
we are about to share.
Through Christ our Lord. Amen.

September 27
To you, O Lord, all honor and glory, for you
are Lord of heaven and earth.
We ask your blessing on all here present and
on the meal we are about to share. Praise be
to you, Lord Jesus Christ. Amen.

September 28
Lord God, bless our home, those around our table, and the meal provided for us with your presence.
Thanks be to God. Amen.

September 29
Lord, we live in your world.
Please bless us and strengthen us for your cause.
In Jesus' name we pray. Amen.

September 30
Lord, bless us this day with nourishment for our bodies.
Bless our hearts and minds, too, that we may know you better and love you more.
In Jesus' name we pray. Amen.

October

October 1
May the grace of God fill our hearts this day
as we ask for God's blessing. Through
Christ our Lord. Amen.

October 2
Praise the Lord at all times, for we have
received the gift of faith.
Praise be to the holy name of God.
Grant us your blessing, we pray.
Thanks be to God. Amen.

October 3
Glory and praise to you, almighty Father,
creator blest.
In your mercy hear your children as we pray
for your blessing. Amen.

October 4
Let us together praise the Lord for he has
blessed us with every good thing.
Praise be to you, Lord Jesus Christ. Amen.

October 5

Thanks be to God for his loving kindness.
He has kept us and provided for us.
To Him be praise forever. Amen.

October 6

Bless us, O Lord, and these Thy gifts we are
about to receive from Thy bounty. Thanks
be to God. Amen.

October 7

O Lord, you are our strength and our
comfort.
We pray for our needs in confidence,
knowing you hear our prayers.
Lord, have mercy on us. Amen.

October 8

Lord, we ask your blessing for all here
present.
Keep us ever close to you. Amen.

October 9

To you, dear Lord, be all honor and glory.
Renew in us a new spirit.
We know God is as close to us as we wish
Him to be.
Praise be to God who loves us and blesses
us. Amen.

October 10

Heavenly Father, accept our thanks this day
for the blessings of home, family, and food.
Thanks be to God. Amen.

October 11

All thanks and praise to you, Lord, for these
loving gifts you have bestowed on this table.
Thanks be to the Lord. Amen.

October 12 - Columbus Day

On this day Christopher Columbus discovered the "new world." He departed Spain and sailed across the Atlantic Ocean, then known as "The Sea of Darkness". After weeks of sailing, a beach was sighted. Columbus gave thanks to God and dedicated the new land to the Lord.

You have blessed this land, Lord. Help us to dedicate our country to you. Amen.

October 13

Dear Lord, we know all good things come from you.

We ask your blessing this day on us and the meal we are about to share.

Thanks be to God. Amen.

October 14

We pray, Lord, that we always remember to thank you for the blessings of peace in our home, for good health and for all you have provided for us.
We give thanks to you, Almighty Father.
Amen.

October 15

Lord, bless us we pray and the meal we are about to share.
In Jesus' name. Amen.

October 16

Thanks be to God for the blessing of family around our table and for the meal we shall share. Amen.

October 17

Our heavenly Father in heaven, bless us as we have our evening meal. Amen.

October 18
Bless us O Lord and these generous gifts of
food we are about to receive.
We ask your forgiveness, Lord, if we have
been lacking in understanding this day.
Amen.

October 19
Dear Lord, we ask for your blessing on all
here present.
We are thankful for your goodness to us.
Amen.

October 20
Holy Spirit, One God, enlighten us that we
may live according to your Word.
We ask your blessing on us and on the meal
we are about to share.
Thanks be to God. Amen.

October 21

We give thanks, Lord, for the meal provided for us this day.
We ask for your blessing through Christ our Lord. Amen.

October 22

May the grace and peace of God be with all of us this day.
Bless us, we pray, Lord and the meal we are about to share. Amen.

October 23

Lord God, You strengthen us through prayer and bring us closer to you. Amen.

October 24

Lord God, teach us your ways that we may walk with you, always knowing that you love us.
Thanks be to God. Amen.

October 25
God, help us all to follow your blessed son,
Jesus.
In good times and bad we must
acknowledge we are Christians.
Bless us with strength to defend our faith.
Amen.

October 26
Lord God of all, creator of the universe, look
down on us gathered at this meal.
In your infinite mercy, bless us we pray.
You are great, but we are small.
Thanks be to God. Amen.

October 27
Tonight we pray for all those who dine alone
and are weary.
Comfort them with your grace, dear Lord.
Have mercy on them, we pray.
Amen.

October 28
Dear God, teach us to be easy to live with and not careless of others.
As we share in your love, let us share in the caring of those we love. Amen

October 29
God loves a cheerful heart as well as a cheerful giver.
Bless the smiling faces, Lord, they are as blooming flowers on a rainy day.
Thanks be to God. Amen.

October 30
Dear Lord, may your Word shine in our hearts.
We are thankful for our blessings and pray we will be worthy of your love. Amen.

October 31

Lord God, tonight is All Hallows Eve. We pray for your light to guide the little goblins and ghosts as they celebrate throughout our neighborhoods.

Keep them safe.

Amen.

November

November 1

May the Holy Spirit be with us as we partake of this meal.
We thank you, Heavenly Father, for your daily care of us.
Glory be to God. Amen.

November 2

Please accept our thanks, Dear Lord, for this food.
Keep us from sin and harm.
We beseech you, O Lord. Amen.

November 3

Thanks be to God for all His blessings.
Keep us ever mindful of His care and love.
Amen.

November 4

O Lord, each day you provide for our needs.
Make us worthy of your attention and care.
Amen.

November 5
The Lord is our Shepherd, we shall not
want.
He has provided for us in all ways.
Let us be faithful unto Him.
In Jesus' name we pray. Amen.

November 6
Lord, you are ever faithful and generous
with love and comfort.
Hear our prayers, Lord, and bless this meal.
Amen.

November 7
Dear Lord, you supply us with what we
need.
We thank you and pray that we will be ever
faithful.
Glory be to God. Amen.

November 8
Lord, you have blessed us abundantly.
We thank you and praise you.
Keep us ever mindful of your love.
Amen.

November 9
With grateful hearts we thank you, Lord, for
all our blessings.
Bless this gathering around this meal.
In Jesus' name. Amen.

November 10
Heavenly Father, we acknowledge your
everlasting presence and glory.
You provide us with comforts and our daily
bread.
Help us keep and praise your name.
Thanks be to God. Amen.

November 11

We thank you, God, for the memory of those men and women who have lost their lives in the service of our country.
We honor them and thank them for their sacrifice.
We honor also all who have served in the armed forces and thank them for their duty to their fellow man.
We pray also that you will bless us with peace in our land. Amen.

November 12

Dear Lord, you are the source of all goodness. Thank you for Thy blessings on us. Amen.

November 13

Oh Lord, let our prayers be ever faithful to you.
We trust in you for all our needs and wants.
Hear us, God, and grant us peace. Amen.

November 14

Bless each one here today with a clean and forgiving heart.
Keep us close to you Lord, we pray, and provide for our eternal needs. Amen.

November 15

Dear God, we are thankful for all our blessings.
We accept this meal as nourishment for our bodies.
Nourish our souls with your grace.
To Thee we pray. Amen.

November 16

Lord, be present at our table each day as we share the bounty you have provided for us.
Thanks be to God. Amen.

November 17
We thank you, dear God, for our many blessings.
Bless this food and this home and each one of us.
Glory be to God. Amen.

November 18
Dear Lord, accept our thanks and praise for your loving kindness and mercy. Forgive all our sins and continue to provide for our needs.
Bless us with love, we pray. Amen.

November 19
Lord, we acknowledge your gifts to us.
We are blessed with every good thing and we thank you from our hearts.
Let our hearts grow with knowledge and love of you. Amen.

November 20
Dear God, you bestow strength through this food we now partake.
Strengthen also our souls with mercy and love that we may eternally praise your name.
Amen.

November 21
Heavenly Father, we give thanks for all these blessings.
Preserve us with your bounty and your love.
Thanks be to God. Amen.

November 22
Father, we thank you for this food and all the heavenly blessings that you have bestowed upon us.
Strengthen our bodies and humble our souls that we may continue in your service.
Through Jesus Christ, your Son. Amen.

November 23
Dear God, grant to us your heavenly peace
and bountiful blessings as we gather
together and partake of this meal.
Glory be to God. Amen.

November 24
Lord, we lift our eyes unto the skies from
whence comes your help.
To you we pray in times of need.
To you we give thanks and praise. Amen.

November 25
Please accept our thanks, dear Lord, for the
blessings of family, friends and the food that
you have provided for us this day.
All praise be unto you. Amen.

November 26
We thank you, Lord, for the strength to face
each day and the food we need as
nourishment.
Bless us O Lord and Thy gifts to us. Amen.

November 27
All good things come from you, Lord.
For all your mercies and blessings, keep us
truly grateful.
In Jesus' name we pray. Amen.

November 28
May the Holy Spirit abide in us and direct
our paths as we go forth each day. Make and
keep us willing to follow you and keep you
in our sight, we pray. Amen.

November 29
We thank you, God, for this food and ask
you to accept our prayers for the forgiveness
of our sins.
Help us to set a standard from which we will
never depart. Amen.

November 30
Dear Lord, you know that we need strong
bodies and clear minds.
We are nourished by your daily bread.
We consecrate this meal to the Lord and
thank Him for all His gifts to us. Amen.

December

December 1
Lord God, you have blessed us and we thank
you for your loving care.
For all your mercies, dear God, keep us ever
grateful. Amen.

December 2
It is you, O Lord, from whom all blessings
flow.
We thank you and praise you for providing
all we need.
Thanks be to God. Amen.

December 3
We thank you, God, to whom we pray.
We are blessed with health of mind and
body.
Please bless us again this day and the meal
we are about to receive. Amen.

December 4

Eternal God, You are as near as our thoughts and you hear us in words and deeds. Keep us close to you, we pray. Amen.

December 5

Lord, we love you and give thanks for all your goodness to us.
We ask your blessing this day and for this meal.
Through Jesus Christ. Amen.

December 6

We thank you, O God, for this beautiful planet.
Teach us to protect and preserve our earthly home and bring forth its bounty with loving care.
In Jesus' name we pray. Amen.

December 7- Pearl Harbor Day
Let us remember this day, dear Lord, and those who gave their lives to protect this country and the freedoms we enjoy.
Grant them eternal rest with you.
Glory be to God. Amen.

December 8
Bless us this day and these gifts we are about to receive, through Christ, our benevolent savior. Amen

December 9
O God, we thank you this evening for the great gifts of family, friends, love and food. In Jesus' name. Amen.

December 10
Lord, we ask your blessing on our home and family and on the food provided for us this day.
Thanks be to God. Amen.

December 11
Heavenly Father, thank you for blessing all here present and on the meal we are about to share. Amen.

December 12
In your mercy, Lord, bless the gifts of the earth that you have provided for us.
May they strengthen us in mind and body.
Thanks be to God. Amen.

December 13
Lord, we thank you for our daily bread and for all the blessings you have bestowed on us.
We pray that you will nourish our souls with Thy grace. Amen.

December 14
Bless us, O Lord, and these gifts that we are about to receive from Thy bounty.
Through Christ, Our Lord. Amen.

December 15
Dear God, we pray that you will bless us and our meal this day.
We thank you for the loving care of us.
May we always walk in your way, Lord.
In Jesus' name. Amen.

December 16
Heavenly Father, we praise you for your blessings of peace and plenty in our land and in our home.
You have blessed us abundantly and we thank you. Amen.

December 17
Lord, you have filled us with your blessings.
We thank you for what we are about to receive. Amen.

December 18

Hear our prayer of praise to you, Lord, for these gifts.
You have blessed us with companionship, love and food. Praise be to God. Amen.

December 19

Lord, in your tender mercy look upon us as we gather for our evening meal.
Bless us, we pray, and the gracious gifts you have provided for us on this day. Amen.

December 20

Enlighten us, dear Lord, with the gift of faith.
Bless our evening meal.
Through Christ our Lord. Amen.

December 21

Blessed is the Lord of our fathers.
We are His children and we pray to bless us this day. Amen.

December 22

The Lord is near to all who call on Him.
Think of Him and He will be with you.
Let us ask His blessing on all gathered here
for this splendid meal. Amen.

December 23

Come, Holy Spirit, and reside in us as we
join together around this table.
Accept our thanks, gracious Lord, for all our
blessings.
In Jesus' name. Amen.

December 24

O God, You have gladdened our hearts with
anticipation of the anniversary of the birth of
our Savior.
Bless us, dear Lord, with true recognition of
your wonderful gift. Amen

December 25

The Lord is born to us today. He shall be called the Prince of Peace, of whose reign there shall be no end. O God, we thank you for the wondrous gift of your blessed Son. We are forever blessed. Amen

Or

The greatest truth of Christmas is that the Gift has already been given. Amen.

Or

And the Word was made flesh and dwelt among us, and we beheld his glory as of the only begotten son of the Father, full of grace and truth.

John 1:14

December 26

Each day we receive blessings from your hand.

For all your mercies, dear Lord, we give thanks. Amen.

December 27
Guide us, we pray, Lord that we may live according to your Word.
Strengthen us with the benefits of the earth, which you have provided. Amen.

December 28
God is our Father.
He has blessed us with all good things and we thank Him for His loving care of us.
Through Christ our Lord. Amen.

December 29
Be present at our table, Lord.
Bless us and this meal we are about to receive. Amen.

December 30
Lord, you created earth for man and gave him dominion over its fruits.
Strengthen us, O Lord we pray, that we protect and preserve this gift to us. Amen.

December 31

You have protected and nourished us
through the past year and we thank you, dear
Lord, for your loving care of us.
Thanks be to God for all His blessings.
Amen

<u>Prayers and Toasts for Special Days</u>

Anniversary

Congratulations on this day and the best of good wishes for your continued happiness.

Baptism

We give thanks to God for His gift of the Holy Spirit. May this child lead the rest of their life according to this beginning.

Birth

We wish God's blessing on you and your new baby.

Birthday

Congratulations on this your very special day. We joyfully celebrate knowing God guides your way. Happy Birthday!

May God bless you with a Beautiful Day and a Wonderful Year!

God's blessing be with you on this special day. Warmest wishes for a wonderful year!

Celebration

We congratulate you on this happy occasion. May God continue to bless you.

Confirmation

May the blessing of your Confirmation remain with you always.

Engagement

How wonderful to celebrate your engagement and to know His blessing abides in your hearts. Congratulations!

Congratulations on this happy occasion. Our prayers and good wishes for your future of happiness.

Graduation

We congratulate you on this happy occasion and ask God to bless you with good health and good cheer as you walk the pathways of life.

New Home

May God bless your new home with joy and love.

New Year

May the Lord bless us in the New Year with good health, good friends and good fortune.

Retirement

God's blessing be with you on your retirement. May all your days be bright with His love.

Travel

May God grant you a wonderful adventure and a safe return.

Wedding

May you have a long and happy life together. Cherish this day, now and forever.

A note about the author

My mother, Anne R. Ford, was one of seven children growing up during the Great Depression. Her father died suddenly when she was nine years old and her mother held the family together with hard work and a firm belief in God's mercy.

Throughout her life, my mother thanked God for His benevolence and believed passionately that He would always bless her and those she loved.

She wrote this book because she wanted to share her love of God and to help others grow closer to Him.

Anne R. Ford died peacefully at age 92 secure in her faith that God would take her into His arms.

Acknowledgements

This book is mostly a family project. My sisters, Joanne and Jane, provided ideas and advice during the writing of the many prayers while I did the final editing and other yeoman tasks. Thanks also to my son, Gavin, for his valuable input. The concept for and the prayers are, of course, all mom.

Prayers Before Meals could not have gotten to the publishing stage without the technical expertise of my good friend Dave Griffin, author of *Monk In The Cellar* and other fine stories.

Printed in Great Britain
by Amazon